I'M A FUTURE ENVIRONMENTALIST!

Written By
Manisha Nayak

Illustrated By
Eliz Ong

WS Education

NEW JERSEY • LONDON • SINGAPORE • BEIJING • SHANGHAI • TAIPEI • CHENNAI

Published by
WS Education Pte. Ltd.
5 Toh Tuck Link, Singapore 596224

National Library Board, Singapore Cataloguing in Publication Data
Name(s): Nayak, Manisha. | Ong, Eliz, illustrator.
Title: I'm a future environmentalist! / written by Manisha Nayak ; illustrated by Eliz Ong.
Other Title(s): I'm a future scientist!
Description: Singapore : WS Education, [2026]
Identifier(s): ISBN 978-981-98-1038-3 (hardcover) | 978-981-98-1039-0 (paperback)
| 978-981-98-1040-6 (book for institutions) | 978-981-98-1041-3 (book for individuals)
Subject(s): LCSH: Environmentalism--Juvenile literature.
| Environmentalists--Juvenile literature. | Environmentalism--Vocational guidance--
Juvenile literature.
Classification: DDC 363.7--dc23

British Library Cataloguing-in-Publication Data
A catalogue record for this book is available from the British Library.

Desk Editor: Daniele Lee

Printed in Singapore

CONTENTS

Say 'Hello' to Winnie!

Are you a fan of the Earth's natural beauty? Do you feel concerned when you see pollution around you? Do you make an effort to keep your environment clean? Do you spread environmental awareness to others? Well, you may just have the makings of an environmentalist in you!

Environmentalists are people who work to protect and preserve the natural environment. They spread awareness about issues such as the impact of human activities on nature and the importance of protecting the Earth for future generations.

Fancy a career as an environmentalist when you grow up? Read on and get to know all about the enriching world of environmental science!

All the best! Winnie

All About the Environment

The environment is made up of all the living and non-living things around us that interact with one another. The air we breathe, the ground we walk on, the clouds we see in the sky, the plants, animals, buildings and vehicles around us, all make up our environment.

The environment is critical for sustaining life. It provides living things with air, water and food for survival. Preserving the environment is very important for the well-being of all living things.

The environment provides these animals with air, water and food.

Many human actions make the environment unsuitable for living things. For example, many forests are cut down to get wood or to clear land for building factories. This causes animals living in the forests to lose their homes. They may not be able to find food or hide from their predators, and may die as a result.

Littering by humans can lead to the dirtying of the environment. This can be very harmful for the environment and the living things in it.

Animals living in the sea may accidentally eat trash and choke.

Watch how the forests of the world have changed over the years!

Poisonous chemicals dumped into water bodies can cause harm to the people and animals that use the water.

We need to take action to prevent the environment from becoming dirty. Here are some ways in which you can help. Can you think of more?

Let's Clean Up!

What you need

- Trash bags
- Tongs
- Rubber gloves

What you need to do

1. Go to the nearest park or beach with your family or friends.
2. Look for trash on the ground.

3. Put on the rubber gloves and use the tongs to pick up and dispose of the trash safely.

4. You may want to separate objects made of recyclable materials such as glass, paper, metal and plastic. Put them in the correct recycle bins.

5. Make this a regular activity to do with your family or friends.

6. Make a poster to spread awareness about trash among your family, friends and neighbours.

Energy Boost

Ever wondered where the electricity in your power sockets comes from? Electricity is generated in many power stations by burning fossil fuels such as coal and natural gas. When these fuels are burnt, steam is produced, which drives turbines connected to generators. Thus, electricity is generated.

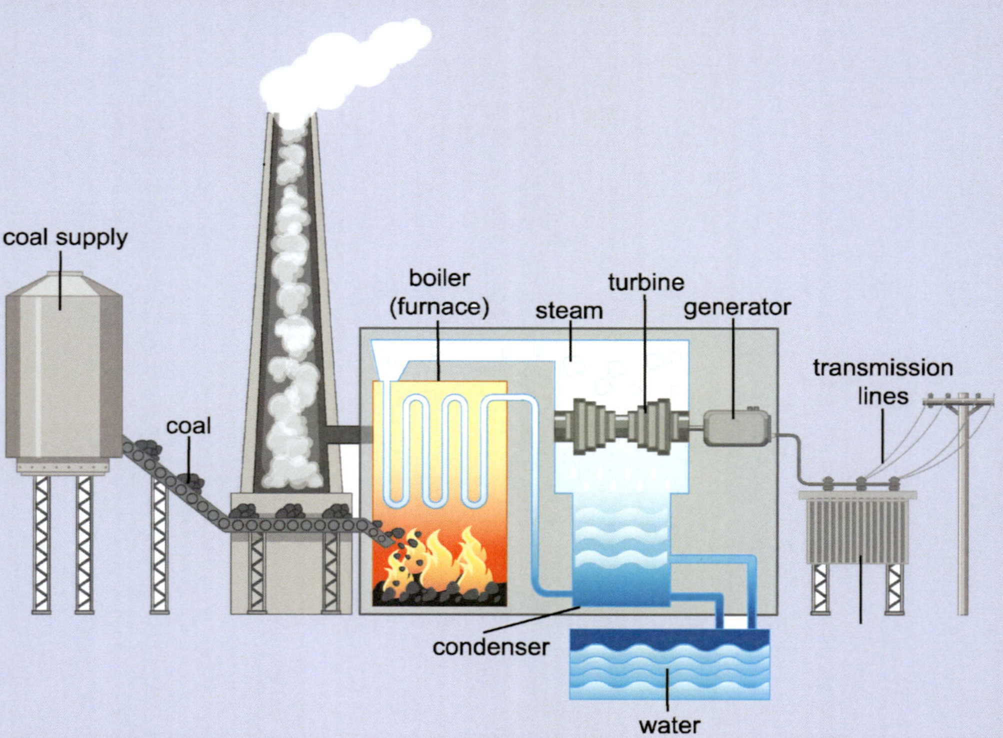

How electricity is generated in a power station

Fossil fuels are named so as they are formed from the remains of animals and plants that lived millions of years ago!

Will fossil fuels run out one day?

Coal is a fossil fuel.

Burning fossil fuels produces gases that are harmful for the environment. Also, fossil fuels will not last forever. They are expected to run out in the near future. That's why they are also known as non-renewable sources of energy.

Many countries generate electricity using alternatives to fossil fuels. These alternatives are known as renewable sources of energy as they are naturally renewed. Some examples are energy from the sun, moving water and wind.

Solar panels use energy from the sun to generate electricity.

A hydroelectric power station uses the energy of moving water to generate electricity.

Wind turbines use the energy of wind to generate electricity.

Did you know that countries such as Iceland, Albania, Nepal, Bhutan and Ethiopia get all of their electricity from renewable energy sources?

Too Hot to Handle!

Do you feel that the weather has been getting hotter and hotter each year? You may have heard terms related to this, such as greenhouse effect, global warming and climate change. Let's find out more!

Greenhouse effect

The greenhouse effect is a natural process that keeps the Earth at a temperature that is suitable to support life. Gases in the Earth's atmosphere, such as carbon dioxide, trap heat from the sun. This helps keep the Earth warm. Without the greenhouse effect, the Earth would be too cold for living things to survive.

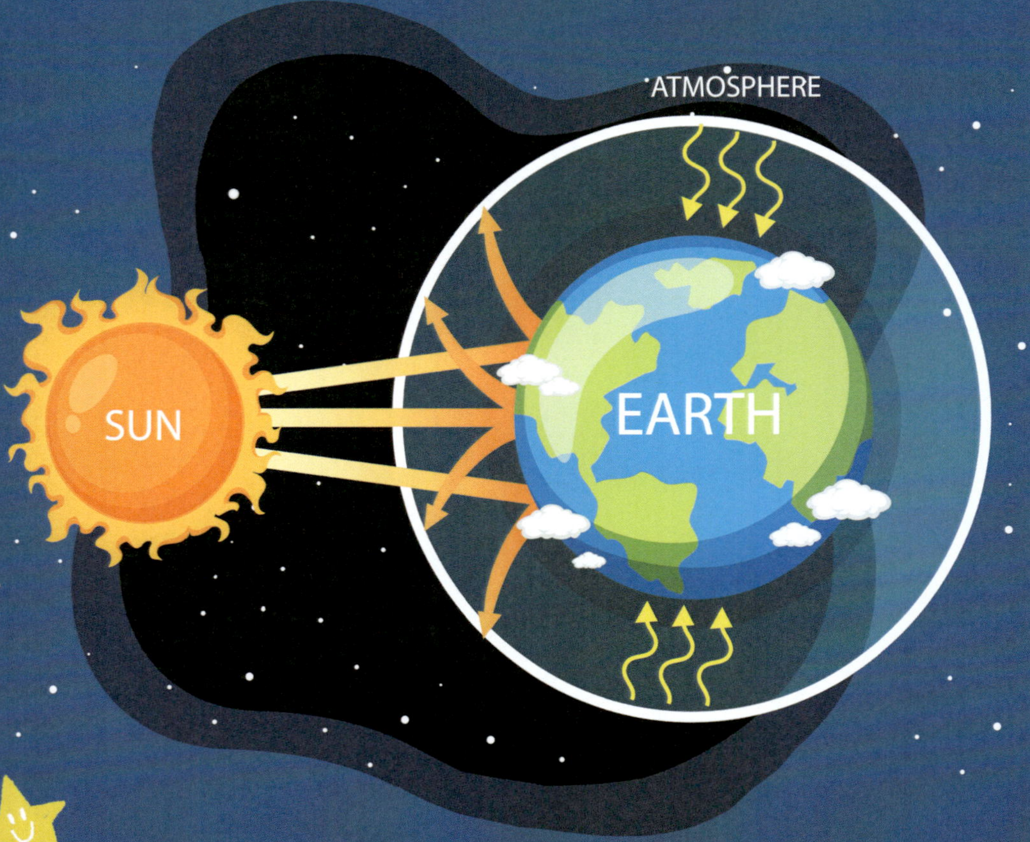

The greenhouse effect keeps the Earth warm enough to support life.

The term 'greenhouse effect' comes from the word 'greenhouse'. A greenhouse is an enclosed structure where plants are grown. Heat trapped from the sun maintains a warm environment inside the greenhouse, allowing plants to grow well.

A greenhouse allows plants to grow under controlled conditions.

Global warming

The natural greenhouse effect is vital for keeping us alive. However, when the greenhouse effect increases, the Earth becomes hotter than normal. This is known as global warming.

Human activities, such as burning fossil fuels and deforestation, lead to an increase in the amount of greenhouse gases like carbon dioxide in the atmosphere. This increases the greenhouse effect, which is harmful for the environment.

Global warming has caused polar ice caps to melt. This has raised sea levels and caused many animals to lose their habitats. Scientists say that many animals may become extinct due to global warming.

Animals such as polar bears are at risk of extinction due to global warming.

WORD WHIZ

extinction: the dying out of all living things of a particular kind

Climate change

Global warming affects atmospheric conditions, ocean temperatures and weather patterns. This leads to extreme changes in the climate. We refer to this as climate change.

Climate change has drastically changed the amount of rainfall in different parts of the world. Some areas experience severe floods, while others experience severe droughts. Extreme weather events such as heatwaves and hurricanes have also become more common.

Oil Ordeal

You may have heard of oil spills and how devastating they are for the environment. What exactly is an oil spill and how does it happen?

An oil spill occurs when a large amount of oil gets spilled in the ocean. This may happen due to many reasons, such as accidents involving oil tankers, pipelines and drilling rigs. The spilled oil covers and spreads over the surface of the water.

Oil spills are very harmful for the environment. The oil coats the bodies of marine animals, affecting their ability to keep warm and find food. The animals may also end up consuming the poisonous oil. Every year, many marine animals die due to oil spills.

When an oil spill occurs, action has to be taken immediately to minimise damage to the environment. This involves massive efforts, such as removing the spilled oil and cleaning up affected living things.

Volunteers cleaning an oil-soaked pelican after an oil spill

Deepwater Disaster

The Deepwater Horizon oil spill of 2010 was one of the largest environmental disasters in the history of the world. Due to an explosion on the Deepwater Horizon drilling rig in the Gulf of Mexico, about 4.9 million barrels of oil spilled into the ocean. Oil continued to leak into the water for 87 days. The clean-up and restoration efforts took more than a decade.

Detective Work

The pictures below show animals that are extinct or endangered. Can you identify them correctly?

Find the answers on page 55!

Trash Talk

We generate a large amount of trash every day. What we throw in our dustbins may disappear from our homes, but it doesn't disappear from the Earth. Do you know what happens to trash after we throw it away?

In some places, trash is disposed of by burning it in an incinerator. In other places, it is collected and sent to a landfill.

A landfill is a place where large amounts of trash are buried in the ground. Over a period of time, the trash breaks down into simpler substances.

There are many environmental problems related to landfills. Trash in landfills may contain chemicals that contaminate the soil and groundwater. It may also produce harmful gases and foul smells. The trash in landfills may take years to decompose.

WORD WHIZ

groundwater: water found under the Earth's surface in spaces in soil and rock

biodegradable: something that can be naturally broken down into harmless substances

As we produce more and more trash, we are also running out of space for landfills.

It is important for us to reduce the amount of trash we generate. This can help us protect the environment.

You can help reduce the trash sent to landfills using the 3Rs — Reduce, Reuse and Recycle.

Learn how Singapore handles its massive amounts of daily trash!

Recycle It Right!

Here are some common items we throw away as trash. Which of these can be recycled?

Aluminium can

Styrofoam box

Glass jar

Plastic shampoo bottle

Ceramic cup

Newspaper

Find the answers on page 55!

The Lost Turtles
Oscar, Olive, the sun's setting. It's time to wrap up our picnic.
Hey, what's this??
Are those... baby turtles??
Yes! They're so tiny... I think they're newly hatched!
Oh no! They're crawling towards the cycling path!

They'll get crushed by pedestrians and cyclists! What do we do??
Should we pick them up and put them in the sea?
No, we shouldn't touch them. They're very fragile.
Let me call Animal Rescue. They're qualified to handle this.

Meanwhile, how do we prevent the baby turtles from going towards the cycling path?
We can't touch them. Maybe we can build a barrier around them using sand?
This is a great idea, Olive!

MAY
Hello, I'm May from Animal Rescue. Thank you for calling me.
Oh dear... These are Hawksbill turtle hatchlings!
Oh! I think I read somewhere that they are endangered!
Yes, we need to do all we can to protect them.
MAY

I see that you've devised a clever way to prevent them from moving towards the cycling path. Thank you for not touching them.
???
What would happen if we touched the hatchlings?
The hatchings are very fragile. Touching them can damage their bodies, stress them and introduce harmful bacteria.
MAY

Picking them up and putting them in the sea can also affect their ability to imprint.
MAY
Ability to *imprint?* What's that?
As turtle hatchlings crawl over the beach to enter the sea, they form a connection with the specific type of sand. This is called imprinting.
MAY

Imprinting is very important for the hatchlings as when they become adults, they will return to the same beach to lay eggs!
Oh... so, picking up hatchlings can prevent them from imprinting!
MAY
Exactly. And this can affect their survival in the long term.

Hey, little fellas. Let me gently guide you towards the sea.
I read that turtle hatchlings use the reflection of moonlight on water as a guide to move towards the sea.
Yes. So why were some of them going in the opposite direction?

Well, sometimes hatchlings mistake artificial lights for moonlight. That can confuse them about where to go.
If they headed away from the sea, they could die of dehydration or get crushed by cyclists. They're lucky that you spotted them.
Thank you! Bye!
The end

I'm Inspired

Often, entire forests are destroyed within a few days. Now imagine how long it would take to *plant* a whole forest! This is what Jadav Payeng, known as the 'Forest Man of India', has managed to achieve.

Over the course of more than 30 years, Payeng has single-handedly planted and taken care of a forest near the Brahmaputra River in India. The forest spans 550 hectares, the equivalent of more than 1,000 football fields!

As a young man, Payeng saw the devastating effect of a flood that washed away many trees near his home.

He decided to take action, starting with planting a small number of trees. He expanded his efforts and over several decades, grew an entire forest!

The forest now serves as a habitat to many animal species, such as tigers, deer, rhinoceroses and monkeys. A herd of wild elephants also visits the forest every year.

The Riveting River

The Singapore River is a bustling centre of activity for both locals and tourists. However, did you know that in the 1970s, the river was extremely filthy and stinky?

Back then, the river was heavily polluted with waste dumped by factories, hawkers and animal farms. Squatters lived along the riverbank without any proper sewage facilities.

In 1977, a master plan involving multiple government agencies was drawn up to clean the river. Foul-smelling mud was dredged from the bottom and banks of the river. Trash and debris were removed.

The Singapore River in the 1960s

Thousands of squatters and hawkers were relocated. Sewage and drainage systems were put in place.

Over time, the water quality improved drastically. The clean-up of the river was officially completed in 1987.

"It should be a way of life to keep the water clean. To keep every stream, culvert and rivulet, free from pollution."

- Lee Kuan Yew
Former Prime Minister of Singapore, 1977

True or False?

Do you remember what you have learnt about the environment so far? Test yourself with this quiz! Which sentences are true and which are false?

1. The environment is made up of non-living things only.
2. Glass, paper, metal and plastic are recyclable materials.
3. Coal and natural gas will last forever.
4. Energy from wind is renewable.
5. Deforestation does not cause global warming.
6. Oil spills can take many years to clean up.
7. If we generate less trash, we can make landfills last longer.
8. Imprinting helps turtles to return to the same beach to lay eggs when they become adults.
9. The 'Forest Man of India' is known for planting an entire forest by himself.
10. It took 20 years to clean up the Singapore River.

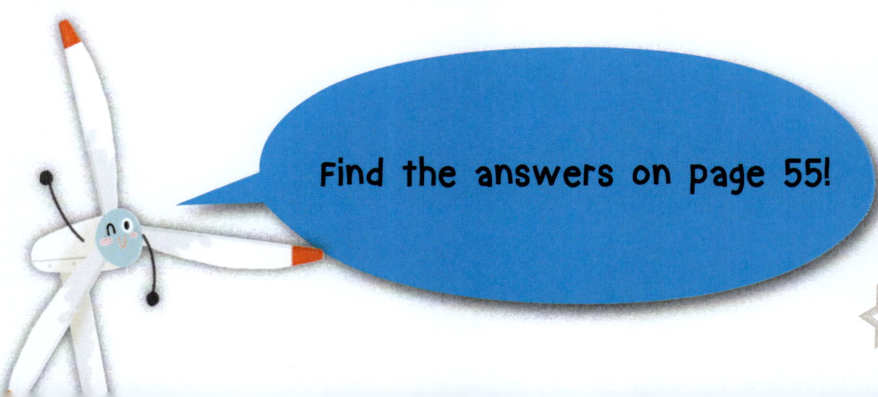

Project Work

Have you heard of 'upcycling'? Upcycling refers to the process of modifying an unwanted object in a way that increases the original object's value.

Let's upcycle an old T-shirt into a tote bag!

What you need

- An old T-shirt
- A ruler
- Adult supervision
- A pair of scissors
- A marker

What you need to do

1. Lay the T-shirt on a flat surface. Cut the sleeves off carefully.

2. Cut along the neckline as shown.

3. Place a ruler across the bottom about 15 cm from the bottom of the T-shirt. Trace it with a marker.

4. Cut strips across the bottom of the T-shirt until the traced line.

5. Tie the first pair of front and back strips into a knot. Knot them again. Continue to knot all the pairs.

6. You will notice a hole between each pair of knotted strips. Close each hole by double-knotting the pair of strips around it.

7. Your bag is ready! You can use leftover fabric from the sleeves to make bows to decorate the handles.

Answers

Detective Work (page 28)

(a) Amur leopard

(b) Sumatran orangutan

(c) Javan rhinoceros

(d) Hawksbill turtle

(e) Iberian lynx

(f) Mountain gorilla

(g) Red panda

(h) Javan pangolin

Recycle It Right! (page 34)

Aluminium can

Glass jar

Plastic shampoo bottle

Newspaper

True or False? (page 49)

1. False	2. True
3. False	4. True
5. False	6. True
7. True	8. True
9. True	10. False

I'M A FUTURE

SCIENTIST!

The I'm a Future Scientist! series of full-colour books for 6–12 year olds will spark sustained interest in scientific fields, such as botany, zoology, marine biology, conservation and the environment, astronomy, and many more, delivering primary-school-level Science learning points in an engaging and relatable way! Through clearly written educational articles, fun cartoons, suggested hands-on activities, as well as full-colour photographs and illustrations, these books are the perfect companions for budding scientists to delve further into a wide range of scientific fields.

WS Education